Ball Python Care

Quick & easy

Colette Sutherland

The author would like to thank Dr. Mark Seward for his help in reviewing this manuscript.

Quick & Easy Ball Python Care

Project Team
Editor: Tom Mazorlig
Copy Editor: Carl Schutt
Design: Patricia Escabi
Series Design: Mary Ann Kahn

T.F.H. Publications
President/CEO: Glen S. Axelrod
Executive Vice President: Mark E. Johnson
Publisher: Christopher T. Reggio
Production Manager: Kathy Bontz

T.F.H. Publications, Inc.
One TFH Plaza
Third and Union Avenues
Neptune City, NJ 07753

Copyright © 2005 by T.F.H. Publications, Inc.

Library of Congress Cataloging-in-Publication Data
Sutherland, Colette.
Quick and easy ball python care / Colette Sutherland.
p. cm.
Includes index.
ISBN 0-7938-1022-1 (alk. paper)
1.   Ball pythons as pets. I. Title.
SF459.S5S88 2005
639.3'9678--dc22
2005008457

This book has been published with the intent to provide accurate and authoritative information in regard to the subject matter within. While every precaution has been taken in preparation of this book, the author and publisher expressly disclaim responsibility for any errors, omissions, or adverse effects arising from the use or application of the information contained herein. The techniques and suggestions are used at the reader's discretion and are not to be considered a substitute for veterinary care. If you suspect a medical problem, consult your veterinarian.

The Leader In Responsible Animal Care For Over 50 Years!™
www.tfhpublications.com

Table
of Contents

Getting Acquainted

Ball pythons are snakes native to western and west central Africa. They are commonly found in scrublands and around cassava farms. The farms have a plentiful supply of African rodents, and the ball python takes advantage of this rich food source. In their home range, ball pythons can be found using abandoned rodent burrows or recently abandoned termite mounds as places of shelter. These types of locations are perfect for ball pythons. Ball pythons are primarily active at night, and they spend the night in search of their prey. The areas of Africa where ball pythons are found experience not only a relatively high level of humidity but also a wet and dry season. Ball pythons breed during the dry season, which also coincides with

The typical ball python is a tan or brown snake with complex black markings. No two ball pythons have the exact same pattern.

the coolest time of the year in their natural range.

The average size of a ball python is 3.5 to 4 feet in length with the occasional large specimen reaching up to 6 feet in length. They are a stout-bodied, muscular python with a well-defined neck and an arrow-shaped head. Five labial (on the lips) heat-sensing pits are found on each side of the upper jaw. These pits are used to sense the body heat given off by potential prey (see page 4 for a picture of the labial pits). Ball pythons—males and females—have spurs that can be found on both sides of the cloaca. The spur appears as a small claw-like structure and is used by the male for courting the female during breeding.

The ball python has a background color of black or dark brown with gold or lighter brown blotches on the sides and along the back. The belly is generally white with occasional flecks of color on the margins. Normal ball pythons are extremely variable in color and pattern. Some may be very light in color while others are very dark. Some will have more striping, while others will appear to be more banded. No two ball pythons will have an identical pattern.

Ball Pythons in the Pet Trade

Ball pythons have been imported into the United States from Africa for decades. The three countries that primarily export ball pythons to the United States are Ghana, Togo, and Benin. Before it is time for wild females to lay their eggs, the local people go out and collect the gravid (pregnant with eggs) females in large numbers. They are then held in captivity until they have laid their eggs. Once the eggs have been laid, they are set up in large areas for incubation. The eggs begin hatching in late March and may continue to hatch through early May. Upon hatching, the new baby ball pythons are exported to numerous countries. The adult ball pythons are generally exported to other countries several months earlier, and some are also released back into the wild. Each year, tens of thousands of ball pythons are brought into the United States. These are the ball pythons that are commonly found in the pet trade.

Through the years, ball pythons have gained notoriety for being bad feeders. Imported adult ball pythons can be difficult to feed in captivity, and many have been known to starve themselves to death. Even imported hatchlings can be problematic, if they have not been properly cared for before they reach the consumer. However, captive-bred ball pythons do not have the same feeding issues. Many wild-caught ball pythons and some captive-bred individuals will go through a fasting period in winter during their adulthood but will resume feeding in the spring or early summer.

The ball python's scientific name is *Python regius*. Translated literally, it means "royal python." In European nations, *Python regius* is referred to as the royal python, while in America the snake is

The "ball" in ball python refers to their defensive behavior of curling into a ball.

referred to as the ball python. The name ball python refers to their habit of coiling into a tight ball with their head securely tucked into the middle of their coils for protection. The ball python belongs to the genus *Python*. This genus contains some of the largest snakes in the reptile world. Other members of this genus are the Burmese python, reticulated python, African rock python, Timor python, blood python, and Angolan python. The ball python is the smallest member of this genus.

The ball python is not a difficult snake to care for. A healthy, well-acclimated import or a captive-bred ball python can make an excellent pet. If you are going to buy an import, you must make sure that he is feeding well and that he has been treated with the proper medications

Scientific Names

You may have noticed that sometimes there are strange looking words in italics that appear after the name of an animal. This is the scientific name, and each animal only has one scientific name. Biologists determine the scientific name of each animal based on what other animals it is related to.

The reason we have scientific names is so scientists all over the world can talk about each animal without worrying about language barriers or other similar animals being confused with the one they want to discuss.

If you use the genus name once, you can abbreviate it to the first letter when you write about it later. So, when I talk about ball pythons again, I could just type *P. regius*. Also, if I wanted to talk about all the snakes in the same genus as the ball python, I would just say *Python* (Note that not all pythons are in the genus *Python*, but they are all in the family Pythonidae).

It is to your benefit to become familiar with scientific names, because hobbyists use them frequently when talking or writing about reptiles.

Quick & Easy Ball Python Care

Best Python

In the United States, ball pythons are one of the most common snakes that people have as pets. Their diversity in colors and their smaller size make them the most desirable member of the python family for the pet owner. .

for internal and external parasites. Captive-bred ball pythons are becoming more readily available each year and with a little effort can be easily found for sale. A ball python's small size and relatively docile temperament make him an excellent choice to keep as a pet. They do have the potential to live for 40 years or more in captivity, so before acquiring one, an individual needs to be prepared for a long-term commitment to the snake. If your circumstances change and you are no longer able to care for your ball python, do your best to find the snake a new owner. Many pet shops will purchase ball pythons from owners that are no longer able to take care of them. There are also many herpetological societies across the United States and Europe. Many of these organizations have an adoptions program and are able to place reptiles and amphibians who are in need of a new home. Do not for any reason release your ball python into the wild.

Where to Buy One

Ball pythons are readily available from a number of different sources. They can be purchased at your local pet shop, at a local reptile expo, or from an Internet vendor. Traditionally, exotic reptiles were only available for purchase at your local pet shop. Then, there began to be small local reptile shows where people could see and purchase many different types of reptiles. Now, with the explosion of Internet businesses, just about any reptile is available at a click of the mouse. Fortunately, the information available to help potential keepers to be successful with their new pet has also increased substantially. Before you buy your ball python, it is well worth your time to read this entire book and then make an informed choice. Keep in mind each potential place to buy a ball python—pet shop, expo, or Internet—has its own pros and cons.

Ball pythons are widely available for purchase on the Internet. You can literally shop dozens of online stores in a very short time. You will find people who breed ball pythons, others who do not breed them but instead broker them, and still others who import them. When possible, buy a captive-bred ball python from a good breeder. Many breeders now offer photos of individual ball pythons that are for sale. This allows you to choose the snake that you like best. Most breeders also offer records that indicate when the snake hatched, how often and on what he has been feeding, the sex of the snake, etc. Many breeders will also be willing to answer any questions that you may have.

Buying a ball python from a local expo reduces your initial cost compared to buying over the Internet, as you avoid paying shipping expenses. Once again, at an expo you will find breeders, brokers, and importers selling ball pythons. One advantage of shopping at an expo is the ability to inspect a wide variety of ball pythons. If you ask to handle one, do not be surprised if the seller requests you to sanitize your hands first with the sanitizer they have with them. This

Along with normal ball pythons, breeders usually have unusual and beautiful varieties (called morphs) for sale, such as this pastel ball python.

Quick & Easy Ball Python Care

is common practice at many expos. Buy from the seller who you feel answers your questions completely and who has the healthiest ball pythons. Make sure to get their contact information in case anything unfortunate occurs or you have more questions at a later date about the snake you purchased.

Local pet shops also offer a variety of reptiles, and many of them carry ball pythons. Here you will have the opportunity to observe an individual snake for potentially a longer period of time than you would at the expo. When you have decided upon which ball python you would like to purchase, ask to see his feeding record or watch him eat before you purchase him and take him home. This is important since one of the biggest complaints with ball pythons is their reluctance to feed. This issue stems from the large number of imported ball pythons from Africa who come into the United States every year.

Purchasing a Healthy Ball Python

When choosing a ball python you will want to handle the snake. Make sure he has good muscle tone and body weight. The snake should feel firm, not limp or mushy. The skin should be clean and smooth. The snake's body should not be triangular in shape, but should have a nice round look. There should not be any sores, bumps, spinal deformities, retained shed skin, or other visible problems. The snake should look alert and flick his tongue while you are handling him.

You will also need to check the snake for potential respiratory problems. While handling the snake you should make sure that the nostrils are clear and that there is no mucus coming out of the mouth. Avoid purchasing a ball python who is wheezing or gurgling, as he most likely has a respiratory infection.

Check the snake carefully for mites and ticks. Ticks are a dead giveaway that you are looking at an imported ball python. Smaller ticks can be dark reddish brown and are found under the scales. Larger ticks, which are often a gray color, can also be found on ball pythons, especially adults. Many times, the larger ticks will be removed by the importer, and the snake will be covered with small wounds and swollen areas where the ticks were removed. Avoid ball pythons with ticks or evidence of previous infestations.

Mites are small black bloodsucking parasites that infest snakes. They can be found around the eye socket, in the labial pits, and in the fold of skin on the bottom jaw of the snake. In a severe case of

mites, you may see the tiny parasites crawling across your hands after handling the snake.

Avoid purchasing snakes with mites. Do not buy an unhealthy ball python with the thought of rescuing the snake. Many times such a purchase will not encourage the seller to take better care of his animals, and it may end up costing you much more in vet bills than what you had previously considered.

Examine a potential pet ball python closely before purchase. You must make sure you are choosing a healthy snake.

Transporting Your New Snake Home

When you have finally selected your pet, make sure that the container or bag you are bringing him home in is secure. Nothing is more disappointing than losing your new snake in the car on the way home. Do not place the snake in an area of the car that is going to allow him to be exposed to the sun. A ball python can overheat quickly when sitting in the sun, and there is the possibility that he may expire. Stopping for a bite to eat on a hot or very cold day may place your ball python in danger. Cars heat up quickly in the summer and cool off fast in the winter. If it will be a long trip home, you may wish to bring an insulated container to place the snake in. This will help to protect him from temperature extremes. If at all possible, go directly home and place your new pet in his cage.

Quarantine

All new ball pythons who are brought into your home should be quarantined for at least 60 days and perhaps as long as 90 days. This is especially important if you already have an number of established reptiles in your home. This process is a must and could possibly save you headaches in the future. Two months is the minimum amount of time for your new arrival to stay in quarantine. It is best, if possible, to house your new acquisition in a different room, away from your established collection. This ball python should be fed last and cleaned last. Your hands must always be thoroughly washed before and after

The quarantine cage should be simple. All that is needed is a water bowl, a hide box, a source of heat, and a plain substrate.

handling your newest snake. During quarantine you will be able to treat your snake for any problems that he may have, such as mites, without exposing your entire collection to the problem. The quarantine setup is roughly the same as the normal setup, but you may want to use plain paper towels or a commercially available cage liner as the substrate. This will allow you to verify that the feces appear normal and not runny or bloody. It will also help you to spot any mites easily. During quarantine, observe your new pet daily for signs of illness, and if any appear, act quickly to remedy the problem.

Housing Your Ball Python

Caging

Ball pythons are a moderately sized snake, and they require a cage that will be large enough to accommodate both them and their cage furnishings. A 30-gallon long terrarium is appropriately sized for an average adult ball python. A long terrarium has a greater floor space than a regular terrarium. A cage that supplies a minimum of 532 square inches of floor space is good for a ball python. Larger specimens will require a larger cage.

Be careful when placing a hatchling in a large enclosure. Many times, a hatchling will refuse to eat due to the stress of all that open space. You may need to purchase a smaller cage to use until the hatchling reaches a larger size or provide plenty of hide boxes in the enclosure.

Not too long ago, the only cages commonly available for reptiles were aquariums with makeshift lids or homemade enclosures. Today, there are dozens of caging choices available for housing reptiles. Not all of the cages available, though, are suitable for ball pythons. Snakes are escape artists, and the ball python is no exception. They will find and exploit any small opening or poorly closed cage. A cage that has its top weighted down with books is not a secure cage. As the snake grows larger, he becomes increasingly stronger, and his ability to push open a top "secured" with heavy objects also increases, to the point where the top will no longer keep the snake inside the cage. This makes it extremely important to purchase secure housing for your snake.

A secure cage provides a safe environment for your snake. You want to keep the snake in and other household pets out. Ball pythons who are lost in a home can turn up almost anywhere. There have even been

No matter how decorative you want your python's enclosure to be, it is critical that you supply a suitable and secure environment. Other considerations are secondary.

Prevent Escapes

The need for secure caging cannot be emphasized enough. Whether your ball python's enclosure is accessible from the front, back, or top, it must be able to be properly secured at all times. If necessary, use small locks to secure the opening of your cage to keep younger siblings and irresponsible friends from gaining access to your snake. Many times these well-meaning individuals will fail to properly close the cage, and your snake will seize the opportunity and escape.

several instances of new homeowners moving into their new home only to find the previous occupants have left something slithering behind! Proper caging will prevent the snake from surprising new homeowners, and it will also prevent the snake from getting out into the neighborhood and causing a media spectacle. Too many times a loose snake has caused panic in a neighborhood, and that has lead to unfavorable legislation against the keeping of reptiles.

When determining what type of cage you would like to use, you will need to take a few things into consideration:

- How many snakes do you wish to keep?

- What is your budget?

- How much space in your home is available for the caging?

- What kind of caging do you prefer (functional, decorative, or a little of both)?

After carefully reviewing your options, you will be better prepared to purchase a cage or cages that will work best for your situation. There are two basic types of caging systems the single-caging system and the rack system.

Single-Caging System

Single caging systems are good for those who only want to house a few snakes. The types of cages available today for single-caging systems are terrariums (commonly found in pet shops), individually produced cages made by a number of online cage manufacturers, and custom-made enclosures (usually made of wood). Terrariums come with a screen top that is secured with a pin. An open top can make it more difficult to keep heat and humidity in the cage. If your climate is such that heat and humidity are not a problem, then a terrarium may do well for you. They are not made to hold water and are consequently lighter than comparably sized aquariums. A quick search on the Internet will provide the consumer with a number of companies that manufacture cages for housing a single snake. There are also very nice custom-made wooden display cages available to house your ball python. Many of these can be used as a piece of furniture, and they also make wonderful conversation pieces. You can find these online or at a local herp show.

Rack System

For those who wish to house numerous snakes, a rack-style system may be the perfect answer. Rack-style systems are designed to hold numerous snakes in their own individual spaces in a fairly compact

Most hobbyists opt for a single-caging system for their ball pythons, often making the cages visually interesting for the keeper.

You can use a lamp or an undertank heater to provide you ball python with heat. Adults need a hot spot that reaches about 90°F.

area. Rack systems are functional in design and are relatively simple to use. Many of them come with built-in heating and thermostats.

Heating

Regardless of which caging system you choose, there are a number of things that are essential for you to provide for your ball python: appropriate temperatures, lighting, humidity, substrate, hide box, and a water dish. Providing your ball python with proper temperatures is a must. Ball pythons need to be kept warm—not hot—in order for them to digest their food properly and remain healthy.

Hot rocks are not a good choice for providing heat for your ball python. There have been too many instances in which a ball python has been severely burned by a hot rock. Undertank heaters are recommended for providing heat for your ball python. Unless your house is going to be very cold or the tank is very large, one undertank heater should be enough to provide your ball python with adequate heat. The undertank heater will require a rheostat or thermostat that will allow you to adjust the amount of heat that the undertank heater produces. In the winter, this mechanism will allow you to increase the amount of heat needed to keep your snake warm as your house cools, and it will also allow you to decrease the amount of heat that is produced in the summer when your home is warmer.

If your home tends to stay relatively cool, it may become necessary for you to add an additional heating element for your ball python. Ceramic heat emitters are an excellent way to increase the ambient air temperature of your enclosure, especially if you are using an enclosure that has a screen top. They do not emit light, only heat, so they can be left on all night. Use of a rheostat with a ceramic heat emitter is also recommended. Always keep fire safety in mind when setting up your heat emitters. Ceramic heat emitters screw into a socket just like a light bulb does. However, they generate much more heat than a light bulb. To prevent the emitter from melting the socket and possibly starting a fire, use a ceramic socket. These can be found at hardware stores and some pet shops.

The ambient air temperature in the cage should be kept between 80° to 85°F. Juvenile ball pythons need a hot spot of around 85°F. Subadult to adult ball pythons need a hot spot of 90°F. Having a hot spot allows ball pythons to control their temperature (thermoregulate) by moving on and off it as they need to. Since ball pythons spend a great deal of time in their hide box, it would be best to position the hot spot under the hide box. If the hide box is too hot, they will not use it. When checking the temperature of the hot spot, be sure you are checking the actual temperature of the substrate above the undertank heater. This can be done conveniently with an infrared temperature gun. Placing a temperature gauge on the side of the tank only measures the temperature of the side of the tank. Keep this in mind when adjusting the heating levels of the cage. Digital thermometers with remote probes can also be used successfully.

Lighting

Ball pythons must be provided with a light cycle or photoperiod. The length of the photoperiod can correspond to the natural lengths of the day and night in your area. The light that enters the room where they

Don't Skip the Thermostat

A temperature control system for your undertank heater is essential for the health of your ball python. A thermostat or rheostat will allow you to adjust the temperatures of the hot spot according to the needs of the snake. This will help to reduce the risk of potential injury to your snake from thermal burns. Providing proper temperatures will also decrease the risk of respiratory infection to your ball python.

are kept should be sufficient, unless the room does not receive sufficient natural light. If there is not enough light in the room to provide your ball python with a definite day and night cycle, you will need to provide your snake with lighting that will fulfill the lighting requirement. You can do this with a low-wattage light bulb or a fluorescent light set on a timer. If you are not breeding your snakes, 12 hours of light and 12 hours of dark is the standard photoperiod.

Humidity

Humidity levels of 50 percent or more are required for ball pythons. This can be difficult to achieve with open screen tops or in places that have relatively low humidity. Winter heating of homes also lowers the level of humidity in the cage. Proper humidity aids in the shedding process. There will be times when the top of the cage will need to be covered to increase the humidity level. It is most crucial to provide an increase in humidity during the time the snake is going to shed. Daily misting (as with a plant sprayer) of the cage during the ball python's shed cycle will help to increase the amount of humidity in the cage.

Substrate

There are many different types of products available on the market today that can be used as a substrate (or bedding) for reptiles, but not all of them are suitable for a ball python. When considering which substrate to use, you will need to take into account the type of setup or "atmosphere" you are trying to create with your snake's cage. If you are going to have a utilitarian setup, then an easily managed substrate will do. Newspaper, cage liners, or other paper-based products are some possible choices that are easy to clean out of the cage and simple to find. Shredded or chipped aspen is commonly used by many individuals. Crushed walnut shells have become more readily available, and they should not pose a problem for your snake. These latter types of substrates lend themselves well to spot cleaning. Spot cleaning is when the soiled area of the cage can be effectively cleaned without the need for changing out the entire substrate.

Sand, corncob bedding, cedarwood products, and some pinewood products should be avoided. Sand can become an irritant to the belly scales of the snake and if swallowed can cause intestinal impaction. Corncob can also cause intestinal impaction in a snake if ingested. The resins in cedar and some poor-quality pine shavings can cause respiratory distress in your ball python and should be avoided altogether.

Some people prefer to use indoor/outdoor carpeting. If you choose to use this as a substrate, have a couple of pieces available. When one becomes soiled, it is easy to remove the soiled piece and replace it with a new fresh one.

Newspaper, aspen shavings, and crushed walnut are all acceptable substrates for a ball python cage. Sand and gravel are not recommended.

Quick & Easy Ball Python Care

Hide Boxes

A hide box of some type is a must for a ball python. This will give the ball python a place to rest and will provide him with the security that he will need. There are numerous styles of hide boxes available to choose from. Some are very simple, while others are more elaborate. Always keep in mind the ease of cleaning when choosing a hide box for your snake. If you do not mind scrubbing out all the nooks and crannies of an ornate hide box, then by all means, provide your snake with one. Make sure the hide box will be large enough to

Ball pythons rarely soak themselves. If yours does so frequently, the humidity in the cage may be too low, or your snake may have mites.

shelter the ball python. Many ball pythons seem to prefer hide boxes that have an opening in the top of the hide box. Ceramic flowerpots may be easily converted into a suitable ball python hide box. The existing hole in the bottom of the pot can be widened. Once the hole is the desired size, make sure any rough edges have been filed or sanded down.

Water Dish

A water dish is also essential for a ball python's cage. It does not need to be large enough for the ball python to soak in, but it does need to be large enough to provide an adequate amount of clean water for your pet. Healthy ball pythons rarely soak in their water dish. If they do try to soak, it is generally a sign of a problem. If there is no hide box in the cage, a ball python who is stressed may use his water dish as a hide box. If the cage is too hot, a ball python will sit in his water dish to try to cool off. The number one reason ball pythons sit in their water dish is mites. As the mites drown, they will accumulate at the bottom of the water dish. Please keep this in mind if your snake begins to spend time in its water dish. If there are no noticeable dead mites floating in the water at the bottom of the dish, this does not indicate that your snake is mite free. Give your snake a thorough visual inspection; if no mites turn up, double check the temperature of the cage and make sure your snake has a suitable hide box. If this doesn't solve the problem it could be possible that your snake does have mites, but they have not yet grown large enough to be easily seen.

Plants

Many people want to have a naturalistic-looking vivarium to keep their snakes in. Plants can be added to a cage with a ball python; however, they will need to be very durable. Hatchling ball pythons will not do too much damage to a plant, but an adult can destroy one. When choosing a live plant, read the label carefully. You will want to avoid purchasing plants that are potentially toxic. There are now many high-quality synthetic plants that are available that can be used to decorate your cage. These are easily cleaned and will hold up better to harsh treatment.

Wood

Pieces of driftwood may also be added to the cage. Before they can be placed into the enclosure, they will need to be properly sterilized. In order to sterilize a piece of wood, it will need to be heated to a temperature of 135°F for 30 minutes. You can do this by wrapping the wood in aluminum foil and heating it in the oven. Any branch or piece of wood added to the cage will need to be fairly sturdy. Once again, ball pythons are a stout-bodied snake and anything placed in the cage will need to be able to support their weight and size as they grow. Ball pythons are not built for climbing. Please keep this in mind when choosing your branch and its placement in the cage.

Cleaning

Now that the cage is furnished, it is ready for its occupant. Eventually, the cage will become soiled. When this occurs it will be necessary to clean the cage as soon as possible. Shed skin should also be promptly removed from the enclosure once it has been discovered. If your substrate allows for spot cleaning, spot clean any

Although ball pythons are considered terrestrial snakes, they have been known to climb both in the wild and captivity.

area that has been soiled. After a couple of months of spot cleaning, it will be necessary to change out the entire substrate that is in the cage. Newspaper or cage liners generally do not allow for spot cleaning. When they become soiled, the entire piece will need to be replaced. If you choose to use indoor/outdoor carpeting, always remember to promptly clean the soiled piece of carpet, so it will be ready the next time you clean the cage. (This is where having a couple pieces of the carpeting comes in handy.)

Before cleaning the entire cage, it will be necessary to remove your snake. Make sure you have a secure place to put your snake while

Branches: Secure and Sturdy

If you want to include branches in your ball python's cage, you must make sure the wood is firmly fixed in place. If it is not, your snake could knock over the branch, possibly getting injured or even killed. Be sure the branches can support your python's weight. Falling from a snapped branch can also injure him.

Housing Your Ball Python

Bleach Is Good and Bad

A mild bleach and water solution is a very effective disinfectant. Always take the time to clearly label your spray bottles with a permanent marker. A careless mistake can cost an unsuspecting ball python his life.

you are cleaning his cage. A snake left unsecured and unattended for a minute is a missing snake!

A mild bleach and water solution (about 10 percent bleach) is very effective at disinfecting the cage. This solution can be mixed and kept in a spray bottle. Be sure to clearly label the spray bottle to prevent it from being used improperly. *Snakes accidentally misted down with bleach and water will perish!* Use the bleach solution to spray all the surfaces of the cage and let it sit for at least 15 minutes. Before placing the snake back into his cage, be sure that there are no damp areas left in the cage and that all of the cleaning solution has been completely rinsed or wiped out of the cage.

If the hide box, water dish, or any decorative feature in the cage has fecal matter adhered to any part of it, the soiled area or areas will need to be thoroughly cleaned. Soap and warm water can be used to clean the cage furnishings. Once again, make sure the object has been thoroughly rinsed and dried before placing it back inside the cage. Also, the water in the water dish should be changed every few days, and the water dish needs to be cleaned on a regular basis also, not only when it gets fecal matter on it.

Handling

Ball pythons can stress fairly quickly if not allowed to acclimate to their new surroundings. Allowing your snake to settle in for a week or more is a good idea. You will need to forgo interacting with your new pet during the adjustment time. Once your snake has begun to feed on a consistent basis, you can then begin to handle your snake.

Quick & Easy Ball Python Care

Many times when ball pythons are handled too much they will refuse to eat. As long as your ball python continues to feed on his regular schedule (except when he is shedding), then you can increase the amount of time you spend handling your snake.

While handling your ball python, be respectful of others; not everyone may share your enthusiasm for snakes. If your friends or family members do not like snakes, do not insist that they hold or touch your snake. Let them decide when they are ready to interact with your snake. Do not take your snake out to public areas, such as the mall or park, where there are lots of people. Taking your snake out into places like this is not in the best interest of your snake. You are only asking for problems.

Shedding

Several times a year your snake will need to shed his skin. Snakes shed their entire skin as they grow and will shed more frequently as rapidly growing juveniles and less frequently as slower growing adults. The shedding process in ball pythons normally takes about two weeks. In the early stages of the process, a ball python's belly will commonly begin to take on a pink hue. As the process progresses, the ball python's skin will become dull and the eyes will cloud over, turning a

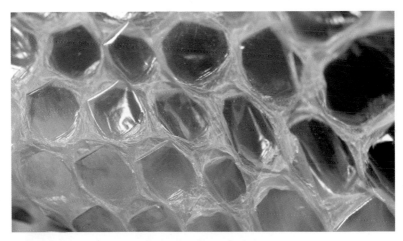

Close-up view of a piece of a ball python's shed skin.

Housing Your Ball Python

gray or blue color. The phrase "in the blue" comes from the blue appearance of the eyes as the snake prepares to shed.

After a few more days the eyes will clear up. In another few days, the ball python will begin to shed his skin. It is important that all the skin comes off. A good shed is when the entire skin comes off of the ball python. It can be in one piece or in a few pieces. Bad sheds happen when there is skin left on the ball python. This is a common sign of low humidity or even possible dehydration. The retained skin will need to be removed. Using a warm damp washcloth and allowing the snake to repeatedly crawl through the cloth will help remove the adhered skin.

The eyes will need to be carefully checked to make sure that there are not any retained eye caps. Do not confuse a "cracked" or dented spectacle (the clear scale that covers the eye) with a retained eye cap. An eye that has a retained eye cap will have a slightly different appearance than the snake's other eye. On some retained eye caps, there will be a small piece of skin that will be noticed around the orbit of the eye. If your snake has a retained eye cap, you will need to use a damp cotton swab and gently rub this over the eye to remove the eye cap. If this does not work, you may need to take your snake to your local veterinarian to have the eye cap removed.

Just as retained eye caps can damage your snake's eye, retained shed skin can damage the skin of your ball python. If your ball python consistently has difficult sheds, you will need to make some more adjustments to the humidity in the cage, and you may also wish to make your snake a shed box. This can be a container with a lid and a hole cut in the side that is large enough for your snake to pass through without difficulty. Inside the box, you can place damp paper towels or damp sphagnum moss. Only use the box during the later stages of shedding, after the eyes have gone clear. Once the snake is done shedding, remove the box, and thoroughly clean it out, so it will be ready to use the next time.

Feeding Your Ball Python

Ball pythons in captivity have been fed a variety of prey items such as rats, mice, hamsters, gerbils, and hatchling chicks. Hamsters, gerbils, and chicks usually are used to entice ball pythons who are reluctant to eat. Once they have begun to feed, it is generally not too difficult to switch them over to more readily available food sources, such as mice and rats. Usually breeders only sell hatchling ball pythons who are already established feeders on either mice or rats.

Many ball pythons will imprint on a single prey item. For example, they will recognize a mouse as a food item but not a rat. There are many ball pythons who will only eat mice their entire lives. Others will only eat rats. Then, there are those who will eat anything that is placed into their cage. Still, others will switch between mice and rats. Since ball pythons will often accept one type of food over another, it is best to feed your ball python what he is accustomed to eating. Be sure to clarify with the person you are buying the ball python from exactly what they have been feeding the snake and how often he has been eating.

A word of caution: In an attempt to save money, do not feed your ball python wild caught rats, mice, or any other wild small animal. Such wild-caught animals may carry parasites that would be harmful or potentially fatal to your ball python.

Food Size and Quantity

It is important to feed your ball python appropriately sized food items. Hatchling ball pythons eat large fuzzy mice or hopper mice. They do not eat pinky mice, unless they are an unusually small hatchling (such as a twin). Oftentimes, when a meal is too large for a ball python, he will not eat it. However, if he is able to swallow the large food item offered, it is possible that it may be regurgitated a day or so later. An appropriately sized food item is one that will

leave a *slight* bulge in your snake. Adult ball pythons who eat mice will need to be offered an appropriate number of mice at their weekly feeding. The number of mice offered will vary depending upon the size of the ball python. Ball pythons 2 to 3 feet in length can be fed two mice at a feeding. Ball pythons who are 3 to 4 feet in length can be fed three or four mice at a

Fuzzy mice are normally the perfect size to feed hatchling ball pythons, but that will depend on how big the hatchling is.

Avoid Wild Food

Under no circumstances should you feed your snake wild rodents, birds, or amphibians of any kind. Doing so could be potentially harmful or even fatal to your ball python.

feeding. These should be offered one at a time and only offered after the previous mouse has been eaten.

Feeding Frequency

Ball pythons can be fed once a week. They should not be offered food while they are in a shed cycle, because most ball pythons will not eat while they are in a shed cycle. After your ball python has eaten, do not handle him for at least 24 hours. This will give your snake some time to begin to digest his meal. If you have fed your ball python a very large meal, you will need to wait longer to handle your snake. If you handle your ball python too roughly or too soon after feeding him, he may regurgitate his meal.

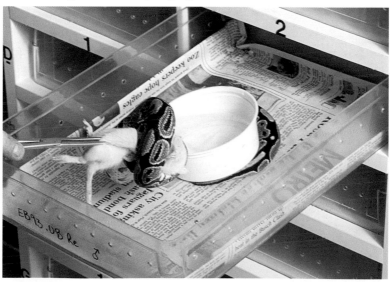

Use a pair of hemostats to feed your ball python; it will prevent accidental biting.

It is best not to disturb your ball python before you feed him. Many times, if a ball python is cleaned or handled before he is to be fed, he will not eat. Feeding a ball python in his cage should not be a problem. When feeding your ball python, it is best to use a pair of 18-inch hemostats or tongs. These are used to place the food item in the cage. Using hemostats reduces the risk of being bitten by your ball python and also reduces the risk of being bitten by an aggressive rodent. Most bites from ball pythons occur during feeding and are due to keeper error.

Pre-killed Food

In many cases, ball pythons can be enticed to feed on thawed or freshly killed rodents. Whenever possible, it is best to feed your ball python dead food. Different stimuli are required to elicit a feeding response in a ball python: heat, movement, and scent. Keep this in mind when switching your ball python over to pre-killed or thawed rodents. It is recommended that you use the hemostats to present the thawed rodent to your ball python. If you choose to offer it by hand, you may have the unfortunate opportunity to be bitten. Remember, your ball python has heat pits that are able to discern relatively small changes in temperature. If your hand is emitting more heat than the thawed rodent, there is a good chance that you will be bitten.

Rodents are easily thawed using warm water or the sun on a nice summer day. If you choose to thaw your mouse or rat outside,

Pre-killed is Better

 Offering your snake pre-killed or thawed rodents is preferable to feeding your snake live rodents. The risk of injury from an aggressive rodent or one left in the cage too long is nonexistent when dealing with dead rodents.

make sure that it is not accessible to crows, ravens, dogs, or the neighborhood cat. Keep in mind that thawing should be done properly to reduce the growth of harmful bacteria. Feeding dead food items eliminates the risk of injury to your ball python from rodent bites. Rodent bites can be very dangerous and even lethal to a ball python. There have been numerous instances in which a live rodent has been left in a cage too long and has done serious and sometimes fatal damage to a ball python. If your ball python will only eat live rodents, do not leave the rodent in the cage for more than five minutes. Since ball pythons eat the entire rodent it is not necessary to provide them with vitamin supplements. They are able to obtain the nutrients they need from their food.

Problem Feeders

With the large number of imported ball pythons that enter the United States every year, it is unfortunately common for someone to buy one and take him home, and have him refuse to eat. There may be many reasons why the ball python may not eat. It could be the time of the year. Many ball pythons will fast during winter. You may be handling the ball python too much. Wild-caught ball pythons need time to acclimate to a captive environment. The temperatures in the cage may not be set properly. Double-check your temperatures to make sure they are correct. Make sure the hide box is the appropriate size for the ball python.

Many ball pythons—even some captive-bred ones—will fast during the winter months. If yours goes off his food during the winter, it is probably no cause for alarm. Just be sure he is healthy.

Once all the husbandry issues have been covered, try different types of prey items. Most imported ball pythons will eat gerbils. If you have gerbils available in your area, offer one to your ball python, and hopefully, he will eat the gerbil. If he appears to be losing weight, you may need to take him to the veterinarian to be checked for parasites and possible force-feeding. Force-feeding is best done by your local veterinarian. The best way to avoid feeding difficulties is to buy captive-bred ball pythons from a reputable breeder.

Breeding
Ball Pythons

Many hobbyist aspire to be breeders. Ball pythons are a good subject for both first-time and experienced breeders. They are not very difficult to breed, yet they have some interesting and complex genetics, allowing the knowledgeable breeder to produce interesting colors and patterns. Before starting your breeding project, you should think about what you are going to do with the young. While most pet stores that deal in reptiles will buy captive-bred ball pythons, you shouldn't expect to get rich by selling them. Until you can sell off the hatchlings, it is your responsibility to give them proper care.

Sexing

Before embarking on your breeding trials, you will first need to determine the sex of the ball pythons that you currently own. There is no way to tell a ball python's sex just by looking at him or her. Both males and females have cloacal spurs. These spurs are found on either side of the cloaca or vent. Spurs do wear down on adult males and can even come off due to an excess of retained shed skin buildup around the base of the spur. Females can also lose spurs in this manner. So, contrary to popular belief, ball pythons cannot be accurately sexed based upon their spur size.

Adult ball pythons are generally sexed by probing, a procedure that involves inserting a specially made metal probe into the vent in the direction of the tail. Male ball pythons will probe to a depth of 8 to 10 subcaudal scales (the scales on the underside of the tail) on average. Females on average will probe to a depth of four subcaudal scales. Please remember that this is a general guideline; some specimens will not probe to the depths indicated. Most reptile

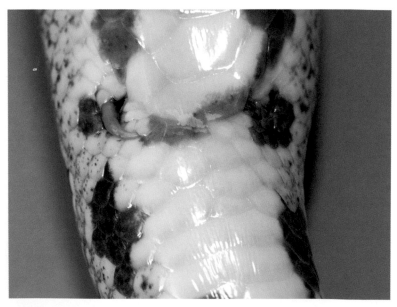

Contrary to popular belief, using spur size to sex ball pythons is not always accurate. Here is a female's spur; note that one has broken off.

Quick & Easy Ball Python Care

Probing and Popping

Ball pythons can't be sexed visually. Probing and popping (or everting) are the two most frequently used methods of sexing snakes. However, both procedures carry some risk of injury. You should have an experienced person show you how to probe or pop your ball python before you attempt to do so yourself.

veterinarians should be able to sex your snake for you, if you have purchased snakes of unknown gender. Most breeders will sell you snakes that have already been properly identified as male or female. Hatchling ball pythons are commonly sexed by manually everting the hemipenes (paired sex organs of the male); this procedure is referred to as popping.

Breeding Conditions

Once you have determined the sex of your ball python or ball pythons, you will need to begin to condition the snake for breeding. First-time males do best when they weigh around 700 grams (about 1.5 pounds), and first-time females should weigh 1,500 grams (about 3 pounds). As females and males mature, they will naturally get larger. Larger females will need to weigh more than 1,500 grams to produce good fertile clutches. The ability of any given female to successfully produce viable eggs is directly linked to the fat she has stored. Too much or too little fat inhibits the ability of the follicles to properly develop.

Once your snakes are the appropriate size, you can begin to consider breeding them. In captivity, ball pythons are considered non-seasonal breeders. This means that they can be bred during any time of the year. Most breeders tend to breed their ball pythons during the winter when the day lengths are shorter and the ambient air temperature is cooler. Do not hibernate your ball pythons; they only require a slight cooling period. It is best to cool your ball pythons for about a month prior to their first breeding attempts. During this

Probing is the most accurate way to sex ball pythons and most other snakes. Do not attempt to probe your snakes until an experienced person shows you how.

time the ambient air temperature can range from the mid-70s during the day to the low 70s at night. The snakes will still need a hot spot at this time. Daytime highs at the hot spot can be 90 degrees with nighttime lows of 80 degrees. Watch the behavior of your snakes. If they are always on the cool side of the cage, turn down the heat a little. Breeding season can begin as early as September and go through May. Normally, ball pythons are bred October through March.

For breeding attempts, males can be introduced into the female's cage or vice versa. During the breeding season, it may be best to breed your ball pythons on a paper product. Occasionally a male may take in a piece of the substrate when he retracts his hemipene. A paper substrate will reduce the risk of a foreign body being taken into the area where the hemipene is retracted. Such foreign objects can cause inflammation of the hemipene and can lead to an infection. If you choose not to breed your snakes on paper, then you should manually evert the hemipenes periodically to make sure there is not debris adhered to them.

Quick & Easy Ball Python Care

Feeding While Breeding

Even though ball pythons experience cooler temperatures during the breeding season, they can still be fed on a regular basis. The size of the food item needs to be smaller due to the decrease in temperature. During this time, it is very important to keep an eye on your breeding male. Males can drop weight fairly quickly during the breeding season and there have been instances where small males have "bred" themselves to death—the male was so interested in breeding, he stopped eating entirely. Larger males may also develop difficulties; some do drop too much weight and begin a downward spiral, refusing to eat and having loose runny stools. Failure to quickly realize that your male is having a problem may result in his untimely demise. Once a female's follicles (sacs on the ovaries where the egg cells mature) have developed past a certain point, she will begin to refuse to eat.

Mating

One male can be used to breed up to five females. It is possible for a male to breed more than five, but five is a more realistic number to work with. Ball pythons will copulate for as long as 24 hours. Before copulation occurs, the male will court the female. Receptive females, whose follicles are beginning to develop, give off the appropriate pheromones that attract the males and stimulate courtship. The male will often climb up on the female and begin to rub her with the lower third of his body. He will also spur the female with his spurs, meaning he will rub the spurs on her body. A female who is receptive to the male will raise her tail or allow the male to raise her tail and attempt copulation. The raising of the tail precedes copulation. Copulation occurs while the tails of the two snakes are entwined. Once copulation is complete, the snakes can then be separated. The pair can be placed back together several times during the breeding season.

Ovulation is the release of the ova (egg cells) from the ovarian follicle. The released ova then move to the oviducts. Ovulation does not last for a long period of time, usually only a day and can easily be missed. This is why it is important to keep the male and the female together for several days during the cooling period.

Fertilization occurs during the process of ovulation. The eggs become shelled after ovulation. When a female ovulates, the lower third of her body becomes distended, making her look as if she has just eaten a large meal. Once the female has ovulated, she will no longer need to be bred by the male. After ovulation occurs, the female will begin to seek out the warmer areas of her enclosure. She may also be found lying upside down or in odd positions in her cage as she thermoregulates. About three weeks after ovulation, the female will go through a shed cycle just before laying her eggs. This is called the pre-laying shed. There will be the occasional female who will not have a pre-laying shed. This is the exception though, not the rule. After the shed, the female generally will lay her eggs in 30 days. If she is kept too cool, it will be longer; if she is fairly warm, it may be shorter. The average is 30 days.

This is a mating between an albino ball python and a spider ball python. Spider is the name given to this particular pattern mutation.

In most python species, including ball pythons, the mother will wrap around her clutch and incubate the eggs.

Egg-Laying

All snakes are individuals, and ball pythons have their share of individuality. Some females will not need a nest box, while others will cruise their cage continuously looking for a suitable place to lay their eggs. For these females, a nesting box should be provided. The box needs to be able to fit into the female's enclosure and should be easily accessible to her and you. The box must be large enough to fit the female comfortably. There should be damp sphagnum moss placed inside the box. Make sure to keep an eye on the moss, so it does not dry out. The moss should be damp, not wet.

The process of laying eggs takes several hours. Oftentimes, the female will begin to lay her eggs sometime in the late evening or early morning. Commonly, the female is found in the morning coiled around her clutch of eggs or just finishing laying her clutch. Upon occasion, a female will lay her eggs during the day. This is the exception, but you never know when you will be the one experiencing the exception. It is always best to check females who are expected to lay their eggs in the morning and in the evening. If the female is discovered in the process of laying her eggs, it is best to let her finish with minimal disturbance. Female ball pythons during and after egg-laying can be fairly aggressive.

Breeders usually incubate ball python eggs on vermiculite or a mixture of vermiculite and perlite.

Incubation

Before the arrival of the eggs, you must decide whether to artificially incubate the eggs or allow the female to incubate them herself. Maternal incubation will work, as long as the female is a good mother. Female ball pythons that are good mothers will remain coiled around their eggs until they begin to hatch. The female will loosen and tighten her coils depending upon how warm or cold the eggs are. She will need to be left undisturbed and at appropriate temperatures and humidity.

The female must be provided with clean drinking water during this time. Placing the water bowl within easy reach of the female will be helpful to her. Female ball pythons have been observed leaving their eggs to get a drink of water, then returning to their eggs when they have satisfied their thirst. The male, if he is housed with the female, needs to be moved into his own cage. Females who are allowed to incubate their own eggs will not feed during this time and may take longer to regain their weight than females whose eggs have been artificially incubated.

When using an incubator, it should be set up and stabilized a week or two before the eggs are due to be laid. It should also be placed in the most temperature-stable room in the home or facility. There are many different commercially available incubators on the market today.

Do not place the probe for the incubator temperature control inside of the egg container. The container with the substrate that the eggs will be placed in should also be in the incubator at this time. This will allow the contents of the container to reach the appropriate temperature and will also allow for adjustments to be made to the size of the container in case it is too large for the incubator. The container should have a lid that allows for easy viewing of the eggs while they are incubating.

The substrate mixture used for incubating ball python eggs can be perlite or a mixture of perlite and vermiculite, available at gardening and home improvement stores. If you decide to use both perlite and vermiculite, make sure the vermiculite mixture has no other additives in it as these may cause the eggs to mold. When using vermiculite and perlite, they can be mixed together using one part perlite to two parts vermiculite. Water will need to be added to the mixture. It is important not to get the mixture too wet; if it is too wet, the eggs may mold and perish. One part water for every five parts of mixture is a good starting point. Adjustments may need to be made to the amount of water added to the mixture, depending upon your local area's humidity. The mixture is important, for it supports the eggs and holds the amount of moisture necessary for the eggs to survive.

Prepare for the Eggs

Stabilizing your incubator a week or two before the eggs are due to be laid will allow you to make any necessary adjustments to the temperature that may be required without harming any eggs. You don't want to have to fiddle with the temperature when the eggs are already in there or have the temperature fluctuate too much. Keep careful track of the temperature in the incubator before the eggs arrive and adjust as needed.

The eggs in a ball python clutch often adhere to each other. The eggs can be left in a clump to incubate.

Removing the eggs from the female can be a tricky business. Female ball pythons are often protective of their clutch of eggs. Some will defend themselves and their eggs quite vigorously. Before taking the female off of her eggs, have a container or pillow case ready to place her inside of. Occasionally a small towel may be placed over the female to help calm her down. You may need to uncoil her tail first. Carefully remove her from the eggs. Try not to let her cling to the eggs too much. Once she has been successfully removed from the clutch, place her in the container or pillow case that has been prepared for her to keep her safe until the clutch has been taken care of.

Take care when moving the eggs. Oftentimes, the eggs will be in a clump. It is important to not drop or let any of the eggs roll around when moving them. If the eggs are in a clump, just place them in the container that way. It is not necessary to separate the eggs. If you feel you must separate the eggs, or it is necessary to separate them so they will fit into the egg container, you can use dental floss to gently separate the eggs.

Fertile eggs are white in color and are about the size of a goose egg. Ball python eggs are not hard shelled like a bird's egg, but are slightly pliant and leathery feeling to the touch. When candled, (the process of holding a small bright light such as a pen light up to the side of the egg) a well-defined vein system along with an embryo can be seen in the egg. If you are lucky enough to catch your female laying her eggs, the embryo will be clearly visible until the shell dries.

Occasionally, it is possible for a ball python to lay an egg that appears to be viable—it has the right color and size—but there is no embryo present. This is an infertile egg. These eggs usually will collapse and mold within two weeks of being placed into the incubator. Slugs (ova that failed to develop) are much smaller than fertile eggs. They are a different color and texture and can be disposed of immediately.

Occasionally, there will be an egg in a clutch that will have one end that did not calcify properly. This end will be brown in color, and the egg may have the shape of a tear drop. These eggs can be incubated with the rest of the clutch. The hatchlings that come from these types of eggs will almost always be much smaller than their siblings and will need to be fed correspondingly smaller food.

Moldy Eggs

If the egg clump has been left intact and an egg begins to get moldy in the center, do not worry too much. If the mold concerns you, you can take some cotton swabs and carefully wipe the mold away from the edges of the other eggs. If the eggs are set out individually in the box and an egg begins to mold and collapse, you can discard that egg. Eggs that begin to get green or blue "water marks" on them are no longer viable and should be removed.

Breeding Ball Pythons

The surface of other eggs in some clutches may appear to be unevenly calcified. As incubation proceeds, these eggs may begin to look like they have dimples all over them. Just maintain proper humidity and temperature and they should hatch with no problem. Once in a while, an egg or two may have a small or large brown spot on the surface. These are called windows and if you have one that is large enough, you will be able to see the developing snake inside of the egg.

While the eggs are incubating, it is important that the temperature remain fairly constant. Since the incubator has been running for a couple of weeks before the eggs arrived, this should be a fairly simple task. Ball python eggs incubate best at 89°F with close to 100 percent humidity. The container will need to be vented every so often to prevent the air from becoming stale inside the egg container. When ball python eggs are incubated too far above their optimum temperature, skeletal deformities of the developing ball pythons can and do occur. Temperatures that are too low often result in fully formed hatchlings that are dead in the egg. The humidity should also be watched closely. If the eggs begin to collapse soon after placing them in the incubator, they may be too dry, and a small amount of water will need to be added to the incubation medium. It is possible to kill the eggs through dehydration.

Be Patient!

Watching a clutch of eggs hatch is always exciting, and the temptation to check on the new hatchlings every few minutes is great. It is important to not excessively disturb the hatchlings; they need the time to absorb the remaining yolk into their body. Hatchlings that have been poked and prodded in the egg too much have been known to rip off their yolk sac. If this happens, the wound needs to be stitched closed.

Quick & Easy Ball Python Care

Ball python eggs start to hatch in about 60 days when kept at 89°F and close to 100 percent humidity.

Hatching and Hatchlings

Approximately two weeks prior to hatching, the eggs will begin to collapse. This is a normal process and should not give you cause to worry. Water droplets will also begin to condense on the top of the egg container as hatching approaches. This is also natural and should not give you concern. The eggs should begin to pip (the slicing of the eggshell by the hatchling) around day 60. Oftentimes, the hatchling snake will make several slits in the egg before he will find one to his liking and poke his nose out. Within a day or two, the entire clutch of eggs should be slit. Baby ball pythons will sit inside the egg for at least a day before they will crawl out. Do not disturb them during this time. They are in the process of absorbing any remaining yolk that has not been used during their development in the egg. The absorption of the yolk is an important process that will provide the hatchling with nutrients to sustain him until he eats its first meal.

Hatchling ball pythons need to be housed in their own separate cages. Failure to house them separately may result in some or all of them refusing to feed. They will need to be provided with a hot spot

One of the most distinctive ball python morphs is the piebald. In this morph, sections of the normal pattern are replaced with pure white. It is a simple recessive trait.

of 85°F and a water dish. In about ten days, they will have their first shed and can be offered their first meal, a fuzzy mouse. If you have access to pinky rats, you could try these, also. Once in a while there will be a stubborn hatchling who will not eat. Provide this one with a hide box and try offering him a very small food item or something different, like a baby gerbil. If all efforts fail and it has been a couple of weeks, it may become necessary for you to assist-feed this hatchling.

Assist-feeding is not force-feeding. It is done with a smaller food item than what the hatchling would normally eat. The rodent is euthanized and gently pressed against the nose of the ball python where the tongue comes out. Once the hatchling has opened his mouth, carefully place the nose of the rodent in the back of the snake's mouth as far as you can. Carefully close the jaws of the hatchling over the rodent and carefully put the snake down. Try not to disturb the hatchling. Nine times out of ten, the baby ball python will eat the food item. Gently pick him up and place him back into his cage. When feeding day comes next, offer him the usual fare; if the snake refuses, you may assist-feed the snake again. Usually, you will not need to assist-feed a ball python hatchling more than a few times before he will begin to readily eat on his own.

When switching your ball python over to pre-killed or thawed rodents, keep in mind that heat, movement, and scent elicit a feeding response. Once the hatchling has developed or demonstrated an aggressive feeding response, it is time to switch him over to pre-killed rodents or thawed rodents. Using a pair of 18-inch hemostats, present the dead food item to the hatchling ball python. You may have to wiggle the food some to simulate movement. If you are using thawed rodents, make sure it is warm enough to elicit a feeding response. Oftentimes, if the thawed rodent is too cold or too hot the ball python will not recognize it as food, and no feeding response will be seen.

Morphs

Ball python mutations are also known as morphs. The majority of the current ball python morphs in the United States were not "created" in captivity. They have been reproduced in captivity, and

Dozens—maybe hundreds—of new ball python morphs are being created by breeders crossing morphs in different combinations. This is a super pastel, the offspring of two pastel parents.

their founding parent or parents were originally brought into the United Sates from Africa were they occurred as a spontaneous genetic mutation in the wild. More than 27 morphs have been brought into the United States from Africa over the past several years, and each year brings the possibility of yet another previously unseen new and unique morph.

It is not uncommon for a breeder to take several years to work out the inheritance pattern of a new mutation. The first morph that was successfully reproduced in captivity back in May of 1992 was the albino ball python. Technically, this is the mutation known as amelanism, as the ability to produce the dark pigment melanin is absent. (See the photo at the beginning of this chapter of the albino ball python).

Designer morphs are created in captivity by breeding different morphs together to produce a new and unique looking ball python. The first of these designer morphs to be produced in captivity was the snow ball python. The snow was produced by breeding together two previously established mutations: an albino (a ball python lacking black pigment) to an axanthic (a ball python lacking yellow pigment). Their subsequent offspring (which all looked normal in appearance, but contained one copy each of the albino gene and axanthic gene) were grown up and then bred back to each other. Since the appearance of the snow ball in 2001, well over 20 new designer ball python morphs have been produced with dozens more on the horizon. With the tremendous number of morphs to work with, the number of potential designer morphs is staggering.

There have also been two hybrids produced using ball pythons. A hybrid is produced when two separate species are bred together to produce a new type of (in this case) snake. There is the blood ball, which is a hybrid between a ball python and a blood python and an Angolan ball, which is a hybrid between an Angolan python and a ball python.

Ball Python
Health Care

Ball pythons do not require regular veterinarian visits or yearly vaccinations like dogs and cats. It is possible to have a ball python who will never need to go to the veterinarian during his lifetime. One of the keys to keeping a ball python healthy is to begin with a well-cared-for, healthy ball python. This makes selecting your original ball python or ball pythons even more important. Choosing a captive-bred ball python who has been properly maintained will provide you with a ball python who initially will have the fewest number of health problems. Keeping the snake healthy will be your responsibility. Providing adequate temperatures in the snake's enclosure and reducing the amount of stress the snake will be exposed to will greatly decrease

Finding a Herp Vet

It is not always easy to find vets who are experienced with reptiles and amphibians. In rural areas, it may be impossible to find one within a reasonable distance. Here are some suggestions to help you locate a vet who can help with your ball python. It is best if you locate one before you actually have an emergency

- Call veterinarians listed as "exotic" or "reptile" vets in the phonebook. Ask them questions to be sure they are familiar with ball pythons.

- Ask at your local pet stores and animal shelters to see if there is someone they can recommend.

- Ask local zoos and animal shelters for a recommendation.

- Herpetological societies are likely to know which local vets treat reptiles and amphibians.

- Contact the Association of Reptilian and Amphibian Veterinarians. Their website is www.arav.org.

the risk of your snake having problems in the future. Proper thermal gradients (a thermal gradient is a range of temperatures for the snake to use from cool to warm) are essential for the health of your ball python. Not all of the commonly seen problems in ball pythons will result in a trip to the veterinarian. For the situations that require veterinarian care, check with your local pet shop for reptile veterinarian recommendations.

Internal Parasites

If the ball python you have purchased is an imported ball python it will be necessary for you to have him checked for internal parasites. Almost all imported ball pythons have parasites, whether they are internal parasites or external parasites (and frequently, they have both). Common internal parasites are flagellates, nematodes, and tapeworms. These can be detected by taking a stool sample to the veterinarian for testing. Prior to collecting the stool sample, it will be necessary to contact your veterinarian to obtain a specimen container for the sample. The brown portion of the stool is the part that will need to be collected, not the white uric acid. Testing for internal parasites is best done on at least two different occasions. Parasites or traces of them are not always shed on a regular basis. One test may come back negative and another done a few days later may be positive. Internal parasites will need to be treated with prescription medication obtained from your veterinarian. Make sure to follow the instructions carefully to insure the demise of the internal parasites.

Ticks

Ticks are also routinely found on imported ball pythons. They are easily removed with a pair of tweezers. The tick needs to be grabbed firmly with the tweezers just behind the head as close to the skin of the ball python as possible. Do not squeeze too hard with the tweezers; you do not want to squish the tick until it has been

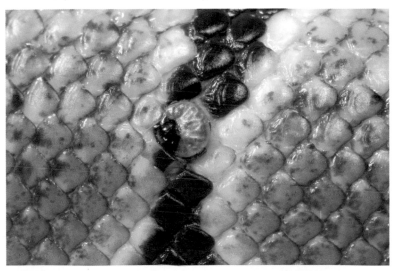

Ticks are blood-sucking parasites that embed themselves between the scales of pythons. If you buy a captive-bred ball python, you are unlikely to encounter ticks.

removed from the snake. Gently pull back and twist the tick out. Treat the area where the tick was attached with an antibiotic ointment. Once the tick has been removed from the ball python, it will need to be disposed of properly. If there are numerous ticks that need to be removed from the ball python, have a receptacle ready to contain the ticks prior to their disposal. This container can be sprayed with your preferred brand of insecticide. Place the lid back on the container after each tick has been dropped inside. The tissue around the eye is fairly delicate and removing a tick improperly from this area can damage the tissue. Your veterinarian should be able to remove any ticks that are embedded around the eye socket.

Mites

Mites are another commonly found external parasite of snakes. They can be found on any species of snake, including ball pythons. Mites are smaller than ticks and move much faster. They are commonly found embedded around the eye sockets of ball pythons or under the chin in the fold of skin that runs down the middle of

Mites can be hard to spot; can you find the one in this picture? Check the folds of skin under your snake's jaw, around the eye sockets, in the labial pits, and in the water bowl.

Quick & Easy Ball Python Care

Mites

Mites are a common yet easily treated external parasite. Once they have been thoroughly eradicated from your collection, strict quarantine procedures must be followed to prevent their reintroduction. Mites can quickly spread to any other snakes you have, so do not delay in getting rid of them. The mites that infest reptiles do not attack birds or mammals.

the bottom jaw. Ball pythons that are heavily infested with mites will sit in their water dishes in an attempt to drown the mites. When a snake who has numerous mites is held, the parasites will be able to be easily seen crawling over the snake and possibly your hand. Mites must be eliminated from the snake and the snake's enclosure. Mites are more than just an irritation; they are a hazard to your snake's health. A ball python may refuse to eat if he is suffering from a large mite infestation. Small ball pythons who are severely infested with mites can die due to blood loss. Mites are easily eradicated through the use of Provent-A-Mite™ or vet-prescribed ivermectin.

Regurgitation

Regurgitation is a serious issue and can be caused by a number of different things, including failure to provide adequate heat, handling the ball python too soon after feeding, feeding a meal that is too large, and gastroenteritis. Gastroenteritis is a disorder of the digestive system, and it can be caused by protozoa or bacteria—both usually signs of poor husbandry. When your snake regurgitates his meal, the temperatures of the cage need to be double-checked to make sure they are appropriate. All other husbandry practices should also be checked to make sure they are correct. After a week offer the ball python a smaller than normal meal with a faunal replacement product (a solution containing beneficial bacteria). If the meal is kept down, the snake can be fed another small meal in a week. Continue to feed the snake small meals for at least a month or two. If the meals are kept down, all should be well. If the snake regurgitates again, a trip to the veterinarian will be in order for some tests to try to determine the cause of the regurgitation. If there are parasites or bacteria present that are irritating the stomach, the veterinarian will be able to prescribe appropriate medications to alleviate the problem.

Failure to Eat

One of the most common health problems experienced with ball pythons is their failure to feed on a regular basis or at all. This is commonly seen with imported ball python adults. When dealing with imported ball pythons, it is best to set them up properly and leave them alone and begin to offer them a variety of prey items. Gerbils generally work best. Once the snake begins to eat, offer him rats or mice.

Long-term captives and captive-bred ball pythons can also stop feeding regularly. There may be a problem if your ball python refuses to feed and it is not winter (many ball pythons will fast during the winter) and your ball python is not a gravid female. Stress is the greatest contributing factor to a ball python not wanting to feed. When dealing with a non-feeding ball python, trying to find the solutions to encourage the snake to feed can be difficult.

To discover the reason why the snake is not feeding, one needs to use the process of elimination. First and foremost, double-check the husbandry of the ball python. Are the temperatures appropriate for

An Ounce of Prevention

When dealing with health issues, the best advice is preventative maintenance. Buying a healthy ball python to begin with and ensuring that he is cared for properly will greatly decrease the number of health issues that you will experience with your ball python.

Overhandling is one of the major causes of ball pythons refusing to feed. If your snake goes off his food, refrain from handling him and make sure no other health issues are present.

the size of the snake? Remember, hatchling ball pythons do not need to be kept as warm as adult ball pythons; they do best with hot spots of 85°F. Is there a hide box? Hide boxes provide a ball python with security and generally are a must-have. Is fresh water available for the snake to drink? Some ball pythons will refuse to feed if they have been without water for a period of time. This can be as short as a few days. Is the ball python being kept in his own tank or is he sharing his space with another ball python? There are times when ball pythons can be kept together in the same cage without any difficulties; however, many times one of the ball pythons will not eat. If this is the case, your snakes will need to be separated and set up properly.

When all the husbandry issues have been checked—and corrected—and the ball python still refuses to eat, then it is necessary to examine other possible causes of the snake not eating. Another one of the biggest causes of a ball python not eating is due to the keeper handling the snake too much. Once your ball python has begun to feed consistently, you can begin to handle your snake.

Start with handling your snake only a few minutes a day. Remember not to handle your snake at all on feeding day. If your snake continues to feed regularly, except while shedding, you can gradually increase the amount of time that you spend holding your snake.

It is best to feed your ball python pre-killed rodents. Live rodents can cause serious injuries to snakes.

When some ball pythons reach weights of 800 to 900 grams, it is not uncommon for them to stop feeding. Oftentimes, this is a very frustrating time. They may not eat for six months or more. When this happens, do not worry. Just be patient and periodically offer the ball python a rodent. Always offer the type of prey the snake was feeding on previously. Once in a while, a ball python will change his food preference from rats to mice or vice versa. Keep this in mind when your snake refuses to feed and everything else appears to be in order. It is also possible for a ball python to begin to refuse food if he has been bitten around the mouth by a rat or a mouse. If this has been the case, it may take some time for the snake to regain enough confidence to resume feeding consistently. Once again, pre-killed or thawed rodents prevent this from happening.

Rodent Bites

Bites from rodents can have serious consequences for your ball python. When a live rodent is left unattended in a ball python's cage, you may be surprised and dismayed by the results. Mice and rats have been known to chew on ball pythons. Chew marks down the backbone and tail are commonly seen. The nails of mice and rats are also sharp. Skin damage can occur to the ball python by the mouse or rat constantly climbing over the snake in its attempts to find a way out of the cage. Severe damage can be caused to a ball python by a hungry rat or mouse—that when left in the cage for either several hours or a day or two—decides to chew on the snake. In cases such as this, it is not uncommon to see areas that have been eaten to the bone all along the backbone or tail region of the snake. In these situations, the snake will require a veterinarian's care. Individual bites from rats may also require a veterinarian's care, depending upon the severity of the bite. Some bites become infected and abscessed. These will need to be excised by a veterinarian and the infection will need to be removed. If at all possible, train your ball python to feed upon thawed or pre-killed rodents.

Thermal Burns

Thermal burns occur when the ball python comes into contact with a surface that is too hot. Thermal burns can be caused by hot rocks that are too hot or undertank heaters that do not have a thermostat or rheostat. Hot rocks are not recommended for ball pythons. The snake will wrap himself around the hot rock in an attempt to warm himself. If the ambient air temperature in the enclosure is too low, the snake will never feel warm. The cool air in the enclosure will keep the snake on the hot rock as he tries to warm himself. The cycle will keep repeating itself until the snake eventually becomes burned. When using undertank heating pads, it is important to use a rheostat or thermostat. This will allow you to adjust the amount of heat that the mat is emitting. In the early stages, burns appear as a reddened area on the belly; this is the area that usually becomes burned. As time progresses, the area may begin to turn brown in color and ooze, and the scales may begin to peel away. Thermal burns require veterinary care. The substrate in the cage, depending upon what is currently in use, should be changed to one that will not stick to the healing wound, such as newspaper, paper towels, or cage liners. Your ball python will go through numerous sheds at this time in an effort to heal the burned area. Your snake may also refuse to eat during this time. Provide the snake with fresh water and keep an eye on him to make sure that he does not dehydrate during his recovery. Follow your veterinarian's instructions carefully while your snake is healing. Thermal burns are most easily prevented through the use of proper heating equipment.

Respiratory Infections

As with people, when they become stressed, ball pythons become more susceptible to respiratory infections. Stress can come in many different forms: not enough fresh water, improper temperatures, too much handling, no hide box, dirty cage, mites, breeding, new cage, etc. Most respiratory infections become noticeable when the snake begins to wheeze when breathing. In severe cases, the ball python

Respiratory infections in ball pythons require veterinary care. Usually, the veterinarian will treat the snake with antibiotics and recommend you raise the cage temperature.

Quick & Easy Ball Python Care

Examine your ball python after each shed to make sure the skin has completely come off. The eyes are the most common places for retained shed as can be seen here.

will sit with his head elevated and in some instances, mucus will be seen smeared along the walls of the cage. The snake will make rather loud gurgling noises as he attempts to breathe. Respiratory infections require a veterinarian's treatment. The temperature of the hot spot in the cage may also need to be temporarily increased to help increase the snake's metabolism during treatment. If your veterinarian recommends raising the heat, follow his advice. As with thermal burns, it will be essential to provide your snake with plenty of fresh water during treatment to prevent dehydration.

Retained Shed

Although a retained shed does not sound like a health problem, it can become one. Retained sheds are a sign of low humidity or dehydration. Several problems can arise from improper shedding. Occasionally, the shed will begin to come off perfectly and begin to "roll" down the snake's body, but it will not roll off all the way. It will stop part way down, the snake leaving a tight "band" of skin around the snake. This band can prevent the snake from eating and can cause decreased blood flow to the areas below the constriction.

Ball Python Health Care

Tail tips that do not shed all the way can have skin build up in the area, resulting in the loss of the tail tip. The tip will become constricted, die, and come off due to blood loss to the area. There may be times when the snake will only shed in patches. The skin left on the snake will need to be removed. If left on the snake and allowed to build up over time, it will cause damage to the scales underneath.

Retained eye caps must also be removed. If eye caps are allowed to build up on the eye, they can eventually damage the eye. Most eye caps are easily removed with a damp cotton swab gently rubbed over the surface of the eye. Make sure there is indeed a retained eye cap on the eye before trying to remove it. If the eye cap is stubborn and will not come off, you may need to take your snake to the veterinarian to have this procedure done. The best way to prevent bad sheds is to provide the ball python with adequate humidity and plenty of fresh water. This does not mean that there needs to be a very large water dish in the enclosure. A modest-size water dish will work fine. Always make sure that there is clean water in the water bowl. In cage setups in which there is a never ending battle to provide adequate humidity, providing your snake with a shed box may be the best solution. A discussion on shed boxes can be found in the shedding section of chapter two.

References

Broghammer, Stefan. *Ball Python: Habitat, Care and Breeding.* Trossingen: M&S Reptilien Verlag, 2001.

Carmichael, Rob. "Maternal Incubation of the Ball Python *Python regius.*" BallPython.Snakes.Net. http://ballpython.snakes.net/robcarmichael/maternal.htm (9 Nov 2004)

Clark, Bob. "Python Color and Pattern Morphs". *Reptiles.* March 1996, pp. 56-67.

Sutherland, Colette. "Genetically Speaking." The Snake Keeper. http://ballpython.com/page.php?topic=genetically (3 Nov 2004)

Resources

MAGAZINES

Contemporary Herpetology
Southeastern Louisiana University
www.nhm.ac.uk/hosted_sites/ch

Herp Digest
www.herpdigest.org

Reptiles Magazine
P.O. Box 6050
Mission Viejo, CA 92690
www.animalnetwork.com/reptiles

ORGANIZATIONS

*American Society of Ichthyologists and
Herpetologists*
Maureen Donnelly, Secretary
Grice Marine Laboratory
Florida International University
Biological Sciences
11200 SW 8th St.
Miami, FL 33199
Telephone: (305) 348-1235
E-mail: asih@fiu.edu
www.asih.org

*Society for the Study of Amphibians and
Reptiles (SSAR)*
Marion Preest, Secretary
The Claremont Colleges
925 N. Mills Ave.
Claremont, CA 91711
Phone: 909-607-8014
E-mail: mpreest@jsd.claremont.edu
www.ssarherps.org

Amphibian, Reptile & Insect Association
Liz Price
23 Windmill Rd
Irthlingsborough
Wellingborough NN9 5RJ
England

WEB RESOURCES

HerpNetwork
www.herpnetwork.com

Kingsnake
www.kingsnake.com

Kingsnake (UK)
www.kingsnake.co.uk

List of Local Herp Societies
www.kingsnake.com/society.html

Resource for feeding issues
http://www.anapsid.org/ballfeed.html

VETERINARY RESOURCES

*Association of Reptile and Amphibian
Veterinarians*
P.O. Box 605
Chester Heights, PA 19017
Phone: 610-358-9530
Fax: 610-892-4813
E-mail: ARAVETS@aol.com
www.arav.org

RESCUE AND ADOPTION SERVICES

ASPCA
424 East 92nd Street
New York, NY 10128-6801
Phone: (212) 876-7700
E-mail: information@aspca.org
www.aspca.org

MARS Reptile Amphibian Rescue
PO Box 65012
Baltimore, MD 21209
Phone: (410) 580-0250
E-mail: rescue@reptileinfo.com

Petfinder
www.petfinder.org

RSPCA (UK)
Wilberforce Way
Southwater
Horsham, West Sussex RH13 9RS
Telephone: 0870 3335 999
www.rspca.org.uk

Index

Note: Boldface numbers indicate illustrations.

Measurement Conversion Chart

UNITS USED IN THIS BOOK

1 gallon = 3.7854 liters

1 inch = 2.54 centimeters

32°F = 0°C (water freezes)

75°F = 23.9°C

CONVERTING FAHRENHEIT TO CELSIUS

Subtract 32 from the Fahrenheit temperature.
Divide the answer by 9.
Multiply that answer by 5.

Photo Credits

Joan Balzarini: 15, 25
R. D. Bartlett: 51
Allen R. Both: 1, 16, 34
Paul Donavan: 23
I. Francais: 5, 12, 14, 29, 30, 31, 38, 44, 57, 58, 60
James Gerholdt: 22
V. T. Jirousek: 18
Aaron Norman: 19
Jorden A. Perrett: 4, 10, 27, 35, 36, 41, 42, 47, 49, 53, 61
Mark Smith: 48
Dan Sutherland: 40, 54
K. H. Switak: 3, 7
TFH Archives: 6